This Walker book belongs to:

_____

_____

_____

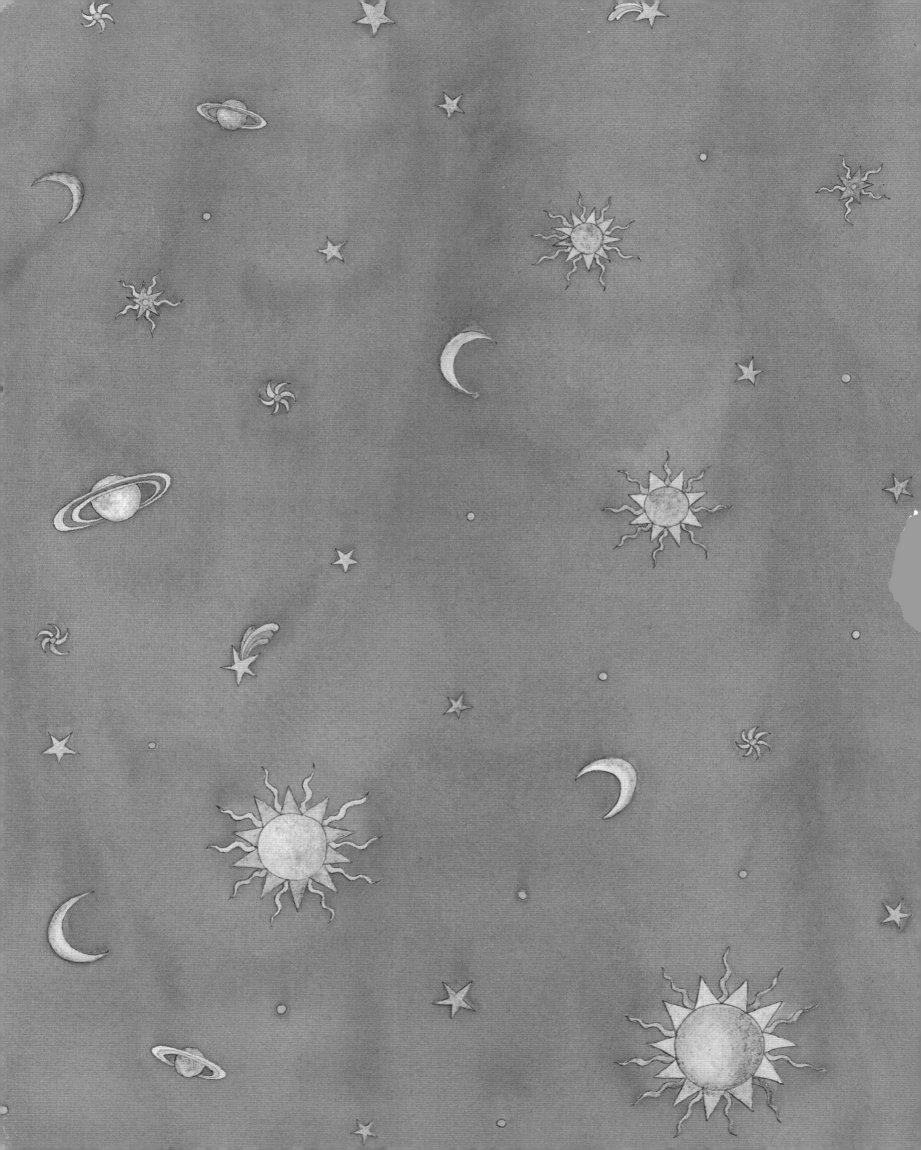

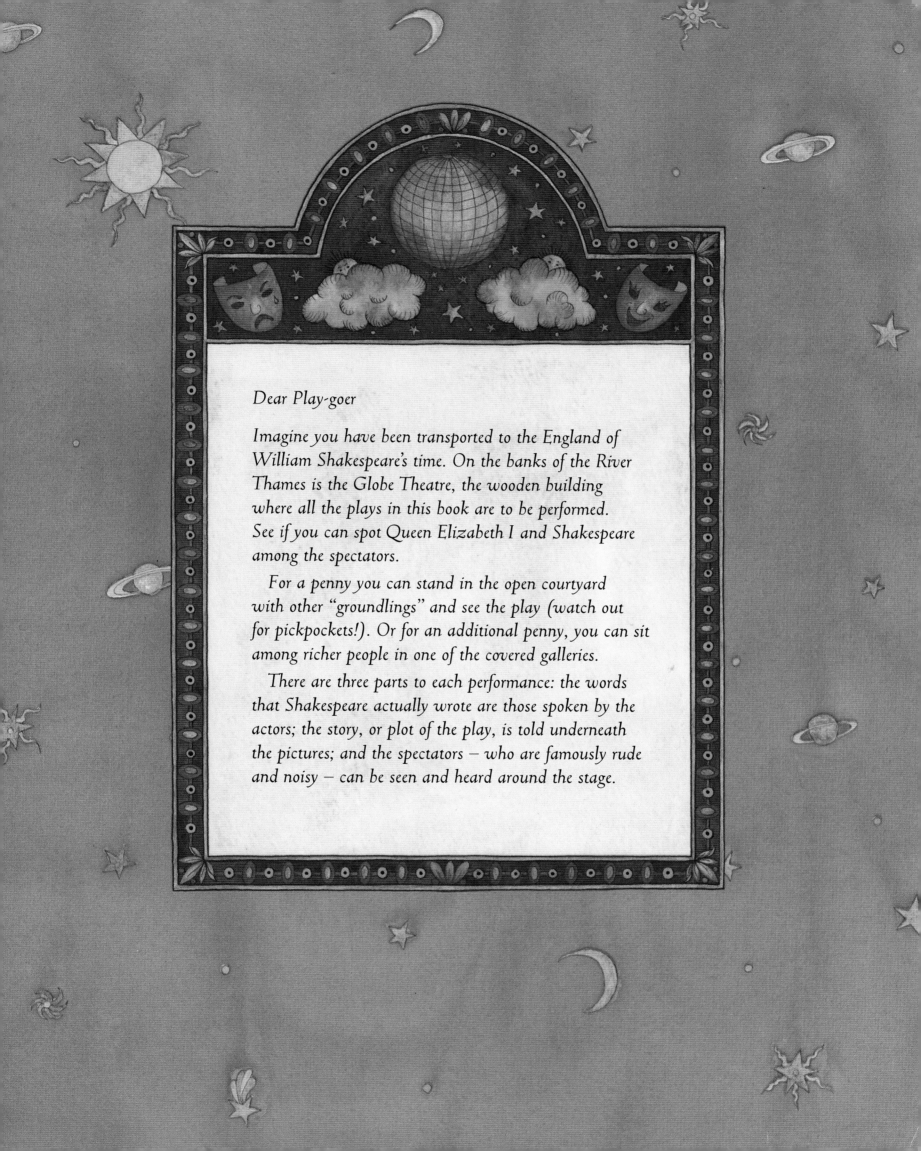

Dear Play-goer

Imagine you have been transported to the England of William Shakespeare's time. On the banks of the River Thames is the Globe Theatre, the wooden building where all the plays in this book are to be performed. See if you can spot Queen Elizabeth I and Shakespeare among the spectators.

For a penny you can stand in the open courtyard with other "groundlings" and see the play (watch out for pickpockets!). Or for an additional penny, you can sit among richer people in one of the covered galleries.

There are three parts to each performance: the words that Shakespeare actually wrote are those spoken by the actors; the story, or plot of the play, is told underneath the pictures; and the spectators — who are famously rude and noisy — can be seen and heard around the stage.

First published 1998 by Walker Books Ltd, 87 Vauxhall Walk, London SE11 5HJ

This edition published 2009

10 9

© 1998 Marcia Williams

The right of Marcia Williams to be identified as author/illustrator of this work has been asserted by her
in accordance with the Copyright, Designs and Patents Act 1988

This book has been typeset in Monotype Centaur and Truesdell

Printed in China

British Library Cataloguing in Publication Data:
a catalogue record for this book is available from the British Library

ISBN 978-1-4063-2334-4

www.walker.co.uk

For Jill

With thanks to Wendy, Helen,
Bridget, Stephanie and Martin

Mr. William Shakespeare's Plays

Seven Plays
Presented by
Marcia Williams

Walker Books
AND SUBSIDIARIES
LONDON · BOSTON · SYDNEY · AUCKLAND

ROMEO and JULIET

Go, sirrah, trudge about Through fair Verona; find those persons out Whose names are written there, and to them say, My house and welcome on their pleasure stay.

I am sent to find those persons Whose names are here writ... I must to the learned.

Do you bite your thumb at us, sir?

In the ancient Italian city of Verona, Lord Capulet was planning a party. He was sure no members of the Montague family would turn up, as the Capulets and Montagues had been feuding for years. The quarrel ran so deep that even their servants fought. But Lord Capulet was wrong.

Is love a tender thing? It is too rough, Too rude, too boisterous; and it pricks like thorn.

Did my heart love till now?

Romeo, Lord Montague's son, and Mercutio, his friend, *did* come — in disguise. He was infatuated with Lord Capulet's niece, Rosaline.

Romeo, however, instantly forgot Rosaline when he saw Lord Capulet's sweet young daughter Juliet. Her beauty stole his heart.

Uncle, this is a Montague!

Young Romeo, is it?

O! She doth teach the torches to burn bright.

'Tis a shame.

He shall be endur'd.

A snowy dove trooping with crows.

The only son of your great enemy.

My only love sprung from my only hate!

Nuts for sale! Eat my fine nuts!

And her only 13.

Unfortunately, Romeo was recognized by Lord Capulet's fiery nephew, Tybalt.

But Lord Capulet forbade fighting at his ball and made Romeo welcome.

So Romeo wooed Juliet and soon their love was mutual, despite the feud.

Will you be my Juliet?

No!

He loves her.

Go on! Kiss her.

As the party ended, Juliet ran to her balcony to declare her love for Romeo to the stars.

Romeo risked death by climbing the Capulets' orchard wall to see Juliet.

That night, the loving pair agreed to wed in secret, lest their feuding families part them.

As dawn broke and Juliet's nurse finally got her to bed, Romeo raced to Friar Laurence.

The friar agreed to marry the sweethearts, hoping this would unite the families.

Later that morning, Juliet joined Romeo at the chapel, and the happy pair were wed.

Then Romeo and Juliet parted, as they knew they must, until Friar Laurence had broken the news to their families.

On the way home, Romeo met his good friends Benvolio and Mercutio, being harangued by Tybalt for consorting with a Montague.

Romeo, now related to Tybalt by his marriage, tried to prevent a fight, but failed.

Tybalt and Mercutio's swords clashed and Mercutio fell dead.

Provoked by his friend's death, Romeo struck Tybalt a fatal blow.

Juliet was carried to the family burial vault, from where, according to the friar's plan, Romeo would rescue her.

But the friar's letter, telling Romeo of the scheme, went astray. A messenger told Romeo the false news of Juliet's sudden "death".

Romeo bought poison and went to the tomb. There he found Paris who, in his misery, attacked Romeo, who slew him in defence.

Then Romeo gave Juliet a kiss and drank the poison. Just too late, Friar Laurence arrived, now aware that his letter had not reached Romeo.

As the friar cried out in horror, Juliet awoke to see Romeo, lifeless beside her.

Hearing voices approach, the friar fled. But Juliet, unable to imagine life without Romeo, took up his dagger and, stabbing herself, fell dead upon her husband's body.

When the families of the Montagues and Capulets arrived upon this tragic scene, they were grief stricken at the consequences of their vendetta. Lord Capulet and Lord Montague vowed to raise a golden statue to each other's child. Thus they buried their feud, along with their precious children, Romeo and his sweet Juliet.

HAMLET
Prince of Denmark

As Hamlet, Prince of Denmark, kept watch with his friend Horatio on the battlements of Elsinore Castle, his father's ghost appeared to him. The dead king told Hamlet that he had been murdered by his brother, Claudius, and urged Hamlet to take revenge.

Gentle Hamlet had idolized his father and was outraged when his mother, Queen Gertrude, married his Uncle Claudius, who then became king. But Hamlet had not suspected his uncle of murder.

Hamlet kept the ghost's secret but all at court, including the king's chamberlain, Polonius, noticed how unstable Hamlet had become.

He often exaggerated his madness, so that his Uncle Claudius and Polonius would not realize that he was suspicious.

Even Ophelia, Polonius' daughter, suffered Hamlet's erratic behaviour. Hamlet's feelings for her fluctuated between tenderness and scorn.

Unable to trust anyone at court, Hamlet felt miserable and confused. Should he take his own life or that of his father's murderer, Claudius?

Hamlet's mother, unaware that Claudius had murdered Hamlet's father, thought his madness was grief for the good king's death.

Polonius was sure that Hamlet's madness stemmed from his love for Ophelia. Only Claudius feared a more sinister reason.

Meanwhile Hamlet's distress grew daily as he watched his mother, so recently widowed, and his murderous uncle together. Yet he hesitated to take revenge without more evidence. Then the arrival of an acting troupe gave Hamlet an idea of how to unmask King Claudius.

Before the assembled court, the actors, on Hamlet's orders, put on a play mimicking the ghost's story of his murder and its consequences. Claudius was so affected by the murder scene that he rushed from the room; Hamlet no longer doubted his uncle's guilt.

Claudius realized that he had been discovered and, hoping to learn more, encouraged Polonius to spy on Hamlet and Queen Gertrude.

From behind the drapes, Polonius overheard Hamlet grow violent when his mother spoke of Claudius as his "father". He cried out in alarm.

Hamlet, thinking it was Claudius' voice, plunged his sword through the drapes, killing Polonius. Anger made Hamlet unrepentant.

Hamlet continued to chide his mother until his father's ghost appeared, urging him to be gentler, but to avenge his death.

Polonius' death gave Claudius an excuse to be rid of Hamlet. Claudius sent the Prince to England with two of his spies, who carried a letter ordering the English to execute Hamlet upon arrival. But Hamlet found the letter and exchanged the spies' names for his own.

On the journey, their ship was attacked by pirates. Hamlet leapt aboard to fight, while his companions fled to England – and their deaths.

The pirates, discovering that they had Prince Hamlet on board, returned him safely to Denmark, hoping for future favours.

At Elsinore, Hamlet was greeted with the news of Ophelia's death. Deranged by her father's violent end, Ophelia had been garlanding a willow tree when she fell into the brook below and drowned. Hamlet was heartbroken. So too was Laertes, who mourned her loss as only a brother can.

In fact, Laertes blamed Hamlet for killing both his father and his sister and he longed for Hamlet's death as much as Claudius did. The pair therefore plotted to kill Hamlet and make his death look like an accident. To this end they issued a challenge to the Prince.

Hamlet was tempted into a fencing match with Laertes, who fought with a poisoned sword instead of a blunt foil. When Laertes drew blood, Hamlet let fly his fury and, in the scuffle, the swords changed hands. Then Laertes too was wounded by his own deadly weapon.

Just then, the queen cried out. Unwittingly, she had drunk from a poisoned cup, prepared for Hamlet by Claudius in case Laertes failed to kill him. Queen Gertrude collapsed on the floor. Hamlet at once suspected his treacherous uncle.

As Laertes lay dying, he told Hamlet that they had both been mortally wounded, and he confessed his part in Claudius' plot.

Reacting to his uncle's fresh villainy, Hamlet stabbed Claudius with the lethal sword, then forced him to drink from the cup of poison.

At last Hamlet had avenged his father's, and now his mother's, murders. As death drew near, he saw Horatio reach for the poison.

Horatio wished to join his friend in death. But Hamlet persuaded him that he must live to tell the true story of Prince Hamlet.

This Horatio did when, moments later, the Prince of Norway arrived. After hearing the story, the prince ordered his cannons to fire a salute. For all who heard the tale knew that, had the fates allowed, Hamlet, Prince of Denmark, would have been a most royal and noble king.

A Midsummer Night's Dream

Once, in Athens, the law decreed that a daughter must marry the man of her father's choice or be punished. Consequently, Egeus had brought his daughter, Hermia, to the court of Theseus, Duke of Athens, for refusing Demetrius, the man of his choice. Hermia actually loved Lysander.

Theseus was sympathetic and gave Hermia four days to choose between love and duty.

Unable to part, Lysander and Hermia told their friend, Helena, they would flee Athens.

So, that very night, they fled to the woods, away from the city and its cruel law.

Meanwhile, Helena revealed their plans to Demetrius because she loved him, and he had once loved her. But Demetrius was now obsessed with Hermia, and set out after the runaway lovers, followed by the love-lorn Helena.

That same night six Athenian workmen went to the wood, to rehearse in secret a play for Duke Theseus' wedding to Hippolyta.

Nearby the fairy king, Oberon, with his sprite Puck, was arguing with Queen Titania over a changeling boy they both wanted.

Oberon, annoyed, planned a trick: he sent Puck to fetch a plant, whose juice made people love the first creature they saw upon waking.

Now, as it happened, Demetrius, with Helena in hot pursuit, passed close to Oberon's hiding place.

Pitying love-sick Helena, Oberon, on Puck's return, told him to anoint Demetrius' eyelids, thinking he would wake to see Helena.

Meanwhile, Oberon found his sleeping queen, Titania. He squeezed the flower's magic juice upon her eyelids.

But Puck mistook Lysander, sleeping near Hermia, for Demetrius and anointed his eyes with the flower's juice.

Then, as luck would have it, Helena, still in pursuit of Demetrius, tripped over Lysander in the dark and woke him!

So, by the flower's magic, Lysander forgot his love for Hermia and fell instantly in love with Helena.

Shocked by Lysander's unexpected love, Helena ran off, pursued by Lysander.

Thus, poor Hermia woke alone. Fearfully, she set out in search of Lysander.

All this while Titania slept on, unaware that the troupe of Athenians, led by Bottom and Peter Quince, had chosen to rehearse their play nearby. It was a perfect opportunity for the mischievous Puck to play one of his tricks, for Titania's eyelids still glistened with magic juice.

Suddenly, at the height of the action, Bottom the weaver appeared wearing an ass's head! The other actors fled in fright. Then Puck, who had transformed Bottom into this ridiculous creature, guided him to the sleeping Titania's side.

When Titania awoke, the first creature she saw was Bottom with an ass's head! Instantly, she fell in love with him. Bottom was not displeased by the attention, especially when Titania ordered her fairies to attend his every whim.

As Puck reported all this to Oberon, Hermia hurried past. Demetrius was close behind but now, exhausted and disheartened, he paused to rest. Realizing Puck's error, Oberon sent him to fetch Helena while he anointed Demetrius' lids with the flower juice.

So when Demetrius awoke and saw Helena, he loved her once again. Helena, far from being happy about this, believed herself mocked.

When Hermia arrived she quickly understood that both Lysander *and* Demetrius now loved Helena. Hermia screamed abuse at Helena.

Puck, on Oberon's orders, drew the lovers on and on until, tired and confused, they fell asleep.

Then Puck anointed Lysander's eyelids in order to restore his love for Hermia.

As Bottom lay sleeping in Titania's arms, Oberon put an antidote on her lids.

Then Oberon woke Titania, who was so mortified at being seen with a snoring ass that she promised Oberon the changeling boy.

Oberon, satisfied at last, danced happily away with Titania, leaving Puck to restore Bottom to his usual self.

As day dawned, a hunting party entered the woods, led by Duke Theseus and Hippolyta; Egeus was also in the party.

When they happened upon the reunited lovers, Egeus was still eager to impose the law of Athens on his daughter, Hermia.

But it was Theseus' wedding day and when he saw the young people back with their original loved ones, he over-ruled Egeus. He bade the party return to Athens and resolved to have all three couples wed that very day: himself to Hippolyta, Hermia to Lysander and Helena to Demetrius. After the ceremony, Bottom and his troupe were called to put on their play, which earned them all a goodly sum and much applause. Then the whole company, at last restored to happy harmony, retired to bed.

That left the way clear for the fairy king and queen, attended by Puck, to bless the palace of Theseus and bid all goodnight – the perfect end to the story, or to a beautifully woven midsummer night's dream in an enchanted wood.

MACBETH

Macbeth and Banquo, two Scottish generals living under the reign of King Duncan, were returning home to Inverness across a bleak heath. They had just bravely defeated an army of rebels much to the delight of the king, who was also Macbeth's cousin.

Suddenly, as if from nowhere, three hideous witches appeared. The first witch greeted Macbeth as Thane (or Lord) of Glamis, which was his correct title. The second greeted him as Thane of Cawdor, which was not, and the third as King of Scotland, an honour held by Duncan.

Just before the witches vanished they also prophesied that Banquo would never be king, but that he would father kings.

As the two generals stood, stunned, news arrived that the king had made Macbeth Thane of Cawdor, in honour of his victory.

With their daggers bloodied, the grooms were blamed. Macbeth, claiming vengeance, killed them both to safeguard his secret.

Despite their display of grief, many suspected the Macbeths of the murder. The king's sons, fearing for their own lives, fled Scotland.

Macbeth, as next in line to the throne, was then crowned king, fulfilling the third prophecy.

Haunted by guilt, but still anxious to retain power, Macbeth worried that Banquo's descendants, not his own, would one day reign as had also been foretold.

So Macbeth resolved to murder Banquo and his son, Fleance, and to this end invited all the local thanes to a feast. As Banquo and Fleance made their way to the palace, they were brutally attacked by Macbeth's hired assassins. Fleance managed to escape, but Banquo died.

Oblivious to this horrific deed, the other thanes were merrily dining when Banquo's ghost suddenly appeared. Only Macbeth could see the spectre and it so unnerved him that the Queen dismissed their guests, lest they wonder at the strange behaviour of their king.

Thereafter Macbeth and his queen began to suffer long, sleepless nights, filled with hideous dreams. Yet Macbeth was still obsessed with not losing the throne, so he returned to the heath to seek out the witches. He found them in a cave, chanting over a cauldron of boiling hell-broth from which three apparitions rose: the first was an armed head, which warned Macbeth to beware of Macduff, the Thane of Fife; the second was a bloody child, who told Macbeth that no man born of woman could harm him; the third was another child, wearing a crown and holding a tree, who reassured Macbeth that he would never be vanquished until Great Birnam Wood came to Dunsinane Hill, where Macbeth's castle stood.

When Macbeth asked if Banquo's heirs would reign, the cauldron sank into the ground and eight ghostly kings passed by, followed by Banquo's ghost. The last king carried a glass which showed many kings, and Macbeth knew them to be Banquo's descendants.

From this day, insecurity plagued Macbeth. So when he heard that Macduff, Thane of Fife, had joined forces with Prince Malcolm, Macbeth ordered the death of Macduff's wife and children. This bloody deed lost Macbeth many friends and determined Malcolm and Macduff to seek revenge.

Then Macbeth received a terrible blow: his queen, who had never come to terms with her guilt and whose nights and days were ceaselessly haunted by ghastly visions, finally succumbed to death. Macbeth felt totally alone. Still more grave news followed…

Thousands of Prince Malcolm's troops were fast approaching, shielded behind branches cut from Great Birnam Wood. Thus it appeared that the wood moved towards Dunsinane Hill and Macbeth's castle, the event predicted to precede Macbeth's downfall.

Macbeth still believed himself invulnerable. Rallying his remaining forces, he waged a bloody war until he met Macduff, face to face. When Macduff disclosed that he had not been born by natural means, but by Caesarean birth with the help of a surgeon, Macbeth knew his end had come.

Now, Prince Malcolm, the rightful heir, claimed his father's throne. Macbeth was dead and the people rejoiced. The wicked reign of Macbeth and his ambitious queen had ended just as had been prophesied. Scotland was at peace, ruled once more by a true and noble king.

The Winter's Tale

One winter, King Leontes of Sicily, Queen Hermione and their young son, Mamillius, were contentedly awaiting the birth of a second child. Polixenes, King of Bohemia, had come to visit and was now about to depart, much against Leontes' wishes.

But Hermione succeeded where her husband had failed, and persuaded Polixenes to stay longer with them.

Instead of pleasing Leontes, this made him insanely jealous. He thought that Hermione and Polixenes must be in love.

King Leontes told Camillo, his advisor, of his belief, wishing him to poison Polixenes.

Unable to change Leontes' mind, Camillo fled with Polixenes to Bohemia.

Meanwhile, Mamillius related a sad tale to distract his mother from the king's anger.

Bohemia ain't got no rotten shore.

Thou art like to have a lullaby too rough.

Watch out! There's a bear about.

Meanwhile, a storm drove the ship carrying Perdita on to the shores of Bohemia. Perdita, with a bundle of keepsakes, was saved, but the ship and all its crew were lost.

Luckily, Perdita was found by a shepherd who cared for her as a daughter for fifteen years.

Aah! It's a tale of sweet romance.

I bless the time When my good falcon made her flight across Thy father's ground.

Prithee, be my present partner in this business.

I willingly obey your command.

Cor, Will's skipped fifteen years!

Perdita was so delightful that Prince Florizel, son of King Polixenes, fell in love with her.

All this time, Camillo was also in Bohemia but unaware of Perdita. Polixenes was angry that his son was courting a shepherdess and asked Camillo to visit her.

As a puritan, I deplore all this.

Contract us 'fore these witnesses.

Come, your hand.

Have you a father?

Thou art too base to be acknowledg'd. Follow us to court.

Ooh! He's in a right pet!

Well disguised, Polixenes and Camillo met Florizel and Perdita and were innocently asked to witness their engagement.

Polixenes suddenly threw off his disguise. He forbade his son to marry a shepherdess and he ordered Florizel to return to court.

Methinks I see Leontes opening his free arms and weeping His welcomes forth.

There is some sap in this.

Most dearly welcome! And your fair princess – goddess!

There are never enough seats!

But Camillo, charmed by the pair, persuaded them to escape to Sicily and beg King Leontes' help, while he sought Polixenes' approval.

King Leontes welcomed Polixenes' son. Alas, Perdita's striking likeness to Hermione brought sad memories flooding back.

FOR HIRE

He doesn't look like a prince.

He's in disguise, you dummy.

I'm a shepherd's daughter.

Baaa!

Well, keep away from princes!

As King Leontes talked of the past, it dawned on the shepherd, who had escorted the pair, that Perdita could be Leontes' daughter. Many rumours flew about as to how this was proven, but it *was* proven and the king was beside himself with happiness.

Leontes took his daughter to see a statue of her mother Hermione, rumoured to be kept by Paulina. In spite of the welcome arrival of Polixenes and Camillo, Leontes could not take his eyes off the life-like statue.

Then Paulina called for music and, to everyone's amazement, the statue began to move. Hermione descended the pedestal. The time had come for the queen to be reunited with her family and friends.

King Polixenes, discovering his son's shepherdess to be a princess, gave his blessing for Florizel and Perdita's marriage, joining the two families in harmony once more. King Leontes gave Paulina's hand in marriage to Camillo, for they held each other in deep affection. Thus ended the strange story of how Paulina had kept Hermione hidden and how Perdita had been found – a wonderful winter's tale to tell by the fireside.

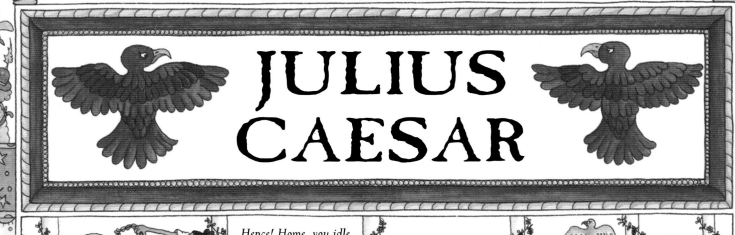

JULIUS CAESAR

It was a day of celebration and the streets of Ancient Rome swarmed with citizens cheering Julius Caesar's victory over his rival, Pompey. At that time, Rome was a Republic — ruled by the people through their Senators. Now some politicians feared that Caesar would want to rule Rome himself.

As Caesar paraded to the games, a soothsayer warned him to beware the Ides of March, or the fifteenth day of the month. Caesar scoffed.

Two Senators, Brutus and Cassius, watched Caesar's triumphant expression. They supported the Republic, and feared Caesar's ambition.

On his return from the games, Caesar did not look so pleased. Casca, a friend of the two Senators, explained what had happened:

Caesar's supporter, Mark Antony, had offered him the crown. Caesar refused it, but to his dismay, the crowd roared its approval!

In raising money for their armies, Brutus and Cassius quarrelled violently. Their friendship and the battle for Rome seemed doomed.

But suddenly Brutus' temper cooled. He confessed that grief had overwhelmed him: his beloved wife, Portia, had killed herself.

As Cassius comforted Brutus, news arrived: Antony and Octavius, having executed many republican Senators, were marching to Phillipi.

The remaining conspirators unwisely agreed to set out for Phillipi and confront their enemies, just as Antony hoped they would.

Drums rolled as dawn broke and the battle for Rome began. All day it raged. But, weakened by the long march to Phillipi, Brutus and Cassius' armies were no match for the enemy. By evening the conspirators had been defeated. Those who had not died in battle fell upon their own swords, rather than witness the fall of the Roman Republic. Octavius was impatient to celebrate their victory but Antony paused to pay his respects to Brutus, whom he knew had been motivated by neither greed nor envy, only by his love for Rome and its people.

THE TEMPEST

Many years ago on a mystical isle, young Miranda and her loving father, Prospero, watched as a ship foundered in a fierce and terrible tempest. Prospero had been preparing for this moment for years, developing his magic powers from a rare book until he could control the elements. Miranda suspected that her father had caused the storm, but had no idea why such a gentle man should wish to harm anyone. So Prospero revealed how he and his daughter had been cast away on the island, twelve years before.

For then thou wast not out three years old.	*Thy father was the Duke of Milan.*	*Me, poor man, my library was dukedom large enough.*	*My brother, and thy uncle, call'd Antonio…*	*did believe he was indeed the duke.*
The king of Naples… hearkens my brother's suit.	*They hurried us aboard a barque;*	*bore us some leagues to sea.*	*Some food we had, and some fresh water.*	*Here in this island we arrived.*

Prospero had been Duke of Milan until his brother Antonio, aided by Alonso, King of Naples, seized power. Prospero and Miranda were set adrift in a tiny boat, but luckily a friend, Gonzalo, had secreted books and provisions on board. These sustained the pair until they drifted on to an island.

The only inhabitants on this isle were the monster Caliban and the sprites his mother had trapped in trees before she died. Caliban became Prospero's servant, as did Ariel, an airy sprite. Ariel, who was invisible to all but Prospero, had been freed from a tree by Prospero's magic and in return had promised to serve him faithfully for twelve years.

As the wise old bear once said, you're never too young for adventure.

I bet he picks his nose.

We like this, already.

When I was little, sprites were two a ducat!

Give us a posy.

Can you see Ariel?

No.

I think Ariel's hidden in the star.

You don't know nothing.

He's right.

Who's right?

I'm right. Ariel's just air.

Know-all.

Prospero told Miranda that the storm-tossed ship carried his old enemies. Then, seeing Ariel approach, Prospero put a plan into action and sent Miranda to sleep.

Ariel spirited the ship's company ashore, isolating all but Antonio, Gonzalo and King Alonso. So the king feared that his son, Prince Ferdinand, must have drowned.

Ariel, now in the guise of a sea nymph, went to fetch Ferdinand to Prospero's cave.

Having dispatched Caliban to gather wood, Prospero then woke Miranda.

Drawn to the cave by Ariel's singing, Ferdinand stared in wonder at lovely Miranda.

The two youngsters fell in love, as Prospero had planned. Adversity, he hoped, would seal the bond, so he accused Ferdinand of spying.

He forbade Miranda to talk to Ferdinand and sent him to shift logs, which Ferdinand did willingly, to stay close to his beloved.

For hours, Ferdinand hauled logs. Miranda never left his side.

Prospero watched Miranda and Ferdinand's love blossom, and finally he relented.

He conjured up a flock of nymphs to sing a blessing on their engagement.

Meanwhile, Caliban gathered driftwood until a looming figure made him hide under his cloak.

It was Trinculo, King Alonso's jester who, fearing a storm, also crawled under the cloak.

Minutes later, Stefano, the king's drunken butler, fell over the heaving bundle.

Trinculo and Stefano were delighted to be reunited. Caliban, unaware of the shipwreck, thought they had dropped from the moon.

Thinking they must be very powerful, Caliban urged the pair to assassinate Prospero. Ariel overheard and flew off to tell his master.

When the traitor Caliban drew near with his companions, Prospero was ready. Ariel had strewn Prospero's finest clothes before the cave.

Caliban, Trinculo, and Stefano crept up, ready to kill Prospero, but were distracted by the array of handsome garments.

When the murderous trio were half dressed, Prospero unleashed a pack of snarling phantom hounds. Driven by Ariel, the dogs chased the rascals far off across the island. Then Ariel returned to aid Prospero: the time had come for him to settle the score with his brother and King Alonso.

King Alonso, Antonio, and the good Gonzalo had been vainly searching for Ferdinand.

Tired and hungry, they were in despair, but then a table of food suddenly materialized.

Amazed, they were about to eat when Ariel, disguised as a harpy, made the food vanish.

Ariel reminded them of their sins against Prospero. Guilt and fear froze their spirits.

Ariel drew them into a magic circle, where they were held like unwilling statues.

Prospero, in his ducal robes, appeared before them as though risen from the dead.

Thy dukedom I resign, and do entreat Thou pardon me my wrongs.

If this prove A vision of the island, one dear son Shall I twice lose.

Antonio and King Alonso were awestruck into true repentance and begged to be forgiven. At last Prospero's anger was placated.

Prospero released them from the circle and led them, and his old friend Gonzalo, to where Ferdinand and Miranda sat playing chess.

A happy ending!

I chose her when I could not ask my father.

Let grief and sorrow still embrace his heart That doth not wish you joy!

Be it so: Amen!

Was't well done?

Prospero's talking to himself again!

King Alonso was overjoyed at finding his son alive and embraced him warmly. Ferdinand told the king of his wish to marry Miranda. Seeing Miranda's beauty and his son's happiness, King Alonso gave his consent. He hoped the union would heal the rift between Milan and Naples.

I think I'll stay in England.

I have been in such a pickle.

I am not Stafano, but a cramp.

I shall be pinch'd to death.

Go, sirrah, to my cell . . . trim it handsomely.

Into the midst of their rejoicing came Caliban, Trinculo, and Stefano, urged on by Ariel. Prospero forgave them too, in return for a little hard labor. The party then made themselves comfortable, while Prospero recounted his adventures of the past twelve years.

Now my charms are all o'erthrown, And what strength I have's mine own.

They all planned to sail to Naples the next morning for the wedding of Miranda and Ferdinand, after which Prospero would return to Milan as its rightful duke. That night, Prospero released his faithful Ariel, who promised him fair winds for their journey. Then Prospero discarded his magic cloak, buried his staff deep in the ground, and threw his book of magic out to sea. After twelve years, Prospero was leaving the enchanted island to Caliban and the sprites. Prospero's tempest had served its purpose, and his dukedom was restored.

Is this a tragedy? — NO! — Is this a comedy? — NO! — Is it a tragicomedy? — Like you! — I do hope I'm appreciated in years to come.

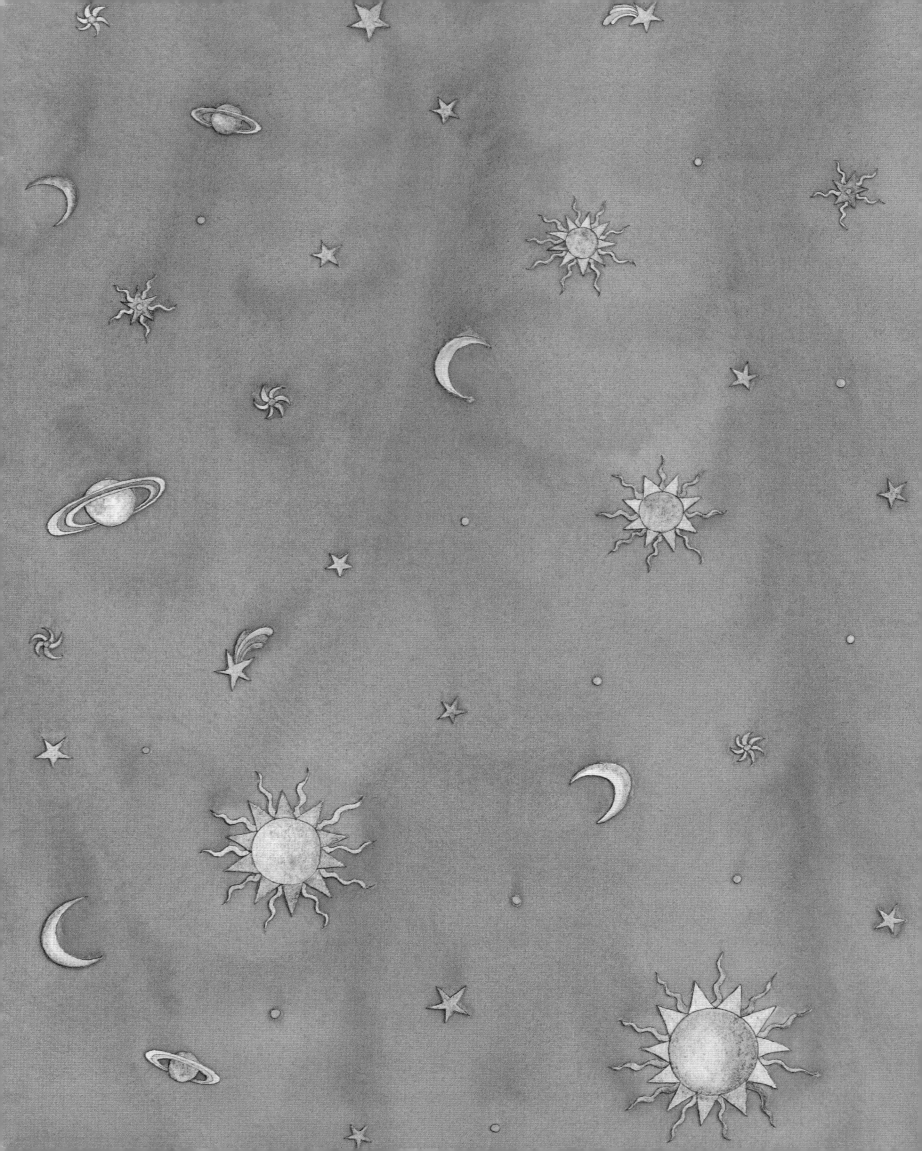

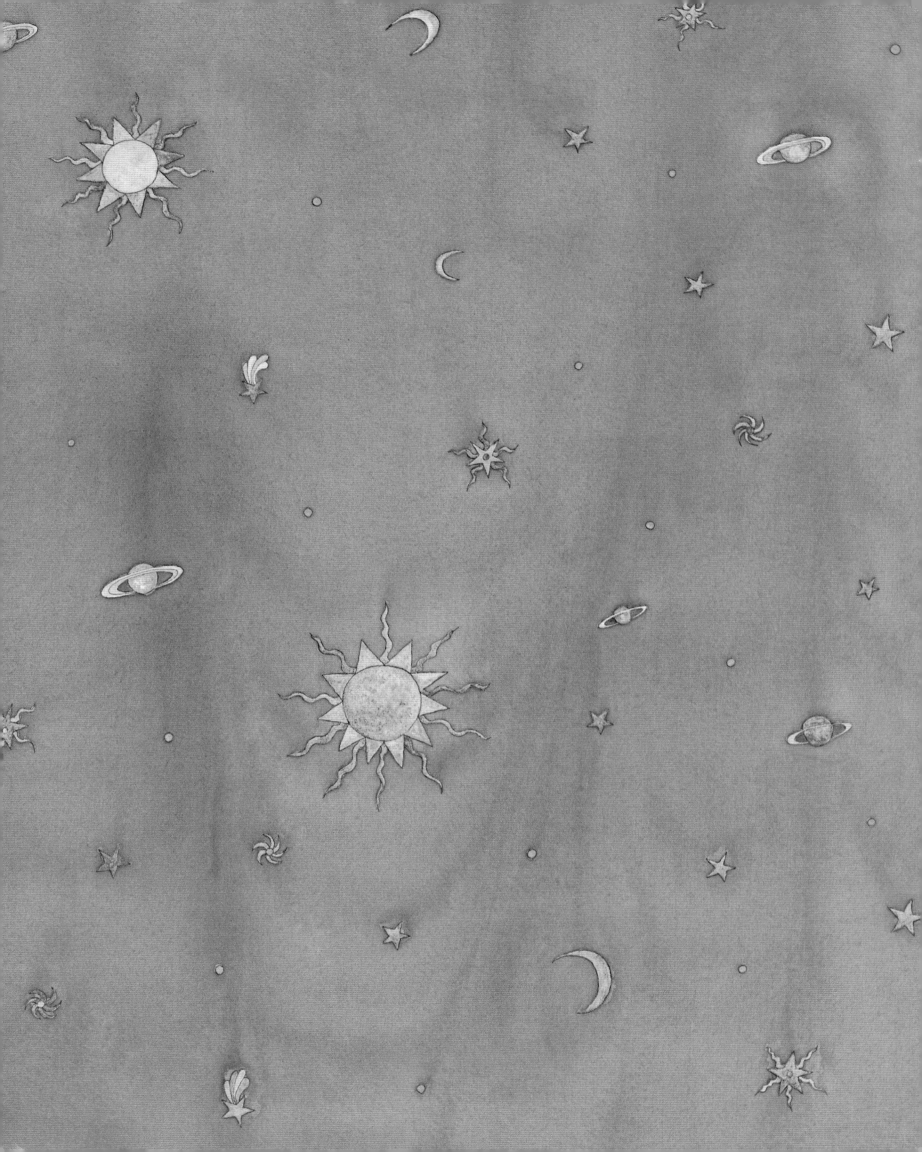

Marcia Williams

With her distinctive cartoon-strip style, lively text and brilliant wit, Marcia Williams brings
to life some of the world's all-time favourite stories and some colourful historical characters.
Her hilarious retellings and clever observations will have children
laughing out loud and coming back for more!

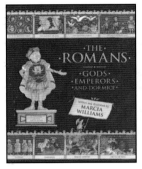

ISBN 978-1-4063-3918-5

ISBN 978-1-4063-4492-9

ISBN 978-1-4063-3832-4

ISBN 978-1-4063-2997-1

ISBN 978-1-4063-2610-9

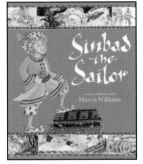

ISBN 978-1-4063-1944-6

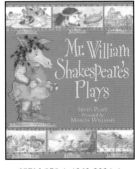

ISBN 978-1-4063-2334-4

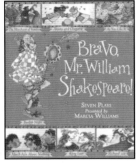

ISBN 978-1-4063-2335-1

ISBN 978-1-4063-0563-0

ISBN 978-1-4063-0562-3

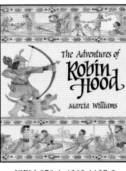

ISBN 978-1-4063-1137-2

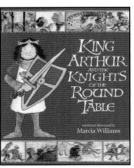

ISBN 978-1-4063-1866-1

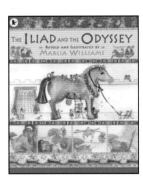

ISBN 978-1-4063-0348-3

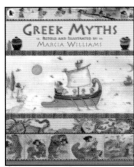

ISBN 978-1-4063-0347-6

ISBN 978-1-4063-0171-7

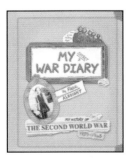

ISBN 978-1-4063-0940-9

ISBN 978-1-4063-1002-3

Available from all good booksellers

www.walker.co.uk